DEDICATION

This play is dedicated to all those who enjoy and appreciate art and culture of other lands and other peoples.

THE GÜEGÜENSE: NICARAGUAN CHARACTER

Author of The Güegüense: First Nicaraguan Character
©Rolando Ernesto Tellez*

First Edition
2010

Publishing Firm
SERFOSA

ISBN: 978-99924-0-962-6

Printed in Nicaragua

*Subsidiary rights—book club, paperback, hardback, reprint, paperback reprint, serial reprint, dramatic, motion picture, television, radio, translation, and other such rights—may be obtained by contacting the author.

etellez43@yahoo.com   ebacca7@gmail.com

Tel. (505)22894596

Introduction

The Güegüense is one of the earliest examples of Native American comedy. As a literature character, the Güegüense has come to represent the mixed identity and consciousness of Nicaraguans, who as individuals struggled to define themselves and resist the hegemonic colonial culture being imposed upon them by the Spanish colonizers. Every year in mid-January, this play is performed in the streets of Diriamba, a town in a region now called "la Meseta de los Pueblos." The comedy-ballet reflects certain typical characteristics of many Nicaraguans regardless their social status.

Sources and acknowledgement

Prior to publishing this booklet of The Güegüense: First Character in Nicaraguan Literature, I read various versions of the play, which included historical background information; I interpreted the texts, deciding which elements from the different versions to use. Later, I revised and adapted the translated script with the help of Americans—native English speakers.

Given the colonial context of this play or street theater, the first Nicaraguan character or Güegüense does not fight using weapons or civil disobedience. This old man character rather uses puns, playing tricks on Spanish authorities. There have been many other interpretations of this street theater in Spanish, and some interpretations have more sexual nuances than others.

This comedy is performed not only by theater groups in Diriamba, but also in other Nicaraguan towns including: Masaya, Granada, and Managua. The play has even been performed in Nicaragua's famous Rubén Darío theater; such performances usually complement other annual religious or non-religious festivities.

Also, I would like to acknowledge Doctor Jorge Eduardo Arellano for kindly letting me use most of the original captions that appear in the play right before the characters speak. I appreciate his contributions to preserve and enhance this invaluable play. Below is one of his articles published in the journal Revistas de Temas Nicaragüenses, No. 7. November, 2008.

The Güegüense: A Proclamation of Human Equality

By Jorge Eduardo Arellano

Two out of forty-three traditional art works declared as Intangible Cultural Heritage by UNESCO, in 2005, were theater plays from Mesoamerica: *Rabinal Achí* from Guatemala and *The Güegüense* from Nicaragua. As it is known, the quiche drama and the comedy in *Espanáhuat* were discovered by the West during the 19th century. The first one was written and translated into French by Charles Etienne de Bourbourg in 1856. The second one was transcribed by Carl Herman Berendt, who mixed two manuscripts in 1874. Thanks to the European anthropologists, it was possible to rescue both pieces. Today, such quiche drama and comedy are universally valued and recognized like the *Kabuki* in Japan and other cultural works: eleven in Asia and Europe; nine in Africa; five in Latin America and the Caribbean; four in Arab countries; and other four of multinational character.

1. A carnival-like parody

Many studies have defined the *Rabinal Achí* and *The Güegüense* as works expressing identity and socio-cultural resistance. One represents the indigenous people of Maya-Quiche—who make up the majority of the Guatemalan population. The other play represents Nicaragua's 17th century indigenous population in la Manquesa, a region contemporarily referred to as the Pueblos Blancos plains.

Both the *Rabinal Achí* and *The Güegüense* plays took place in a sacrilegious context of Catholic Christian rituals and festivities being imposed by Spaniards. The carnival-like characteristics of *The Güegüense*, as an expression of paganism, works as a parody or irony, or natural procedures to express the comedy of human intent, according to Mattew Hogart (1969: 115).

A fundamental technique in satire is degradation or devaluation of a victim by reducing his status and dignity" (Hogart 1969: 115). These procedures and technique are involved in the dynamics of our theater play.

The Güegüense was performed in the Nahuatl theater, which was started and funded by missionaries in the second half of the 17th century. Its farce, dances, and dialogues are classified by the Mexican researcher as "pueblerinos" or town-like (Horcasitas 1974: 11). Created and developed in a colonial period, these dances with dialogues do not have religious themes, but instead include Pre-Columbian elements.

v

2. Indigenous and Spanish roots

Rabinal Achí maintains its indigenous physical characteristics: it hardly shows mestizo elements because of its clothing and the way this play has included both Catholic and Mayan rituals and beliefs (García Escobar 1992: 61). However, *The Güegüense* has indigenous and Spanish roots. For this reason, it has been considered the masterpiece of both popular and mestizo dramatic art in Mesoamerica. It has been considered the first native Hispanic-American play about colonial themes and is foundational in Nicaraguan Literature canon.

"The majority of European literatures," according to Gunther Schmigalle, "begin their historical development with a monumental piece, generally an epic and historic poem: *the Iliad* in Greece, *the Mio Cid Chant* in Spain, *OS Lusíadas* in Portugal, etc. Yet, only *La Araucana* of Chile has been considered an epic poem in Latin America. Although we could debate whether or not Alonso de Ercilla´s work is part of the Chilean or Spanish literature. As opposed to an epic or heroic poem, *The Güegüense*—the first monument of Nicaraguan literature—is a dance comedy, with a satirical and mocking nature (Schmigalle 1944: 120).

3. On the fringes of the colonial discourse

Our theatrical play and musical came to exist outside of the colonial discourse, which can be seen through official expressions: the literature *of the oppressed, the clergy*, the *Creole or native affirmation* and *the eulogy of power* (Arellano, 1994: 136). *The Güegüense* comes from an oral tradition—it was not printed or published, and it was passed on orally even after the Hispanic culture had already influenced the Mesoamerican indigenous populations. The plot can be traced backed to a small, marginal province of the Spanish empire, which was enduring a crisis: this empire needed taxes to survive. This scene clearly reflects a baroque influence in the character's clothing, violin, miming, and musical scenes.

According to Salomón de la Selva, the vivacious dialogue and the baroque influence make the play *precious and unique.* There is no other play like this in Mesoamerica. It serves as an exceptional example of the fusion of Catholic and Mayan beliefs and rituals. The main character or *Güegüense* is a mix of a Pre-Columbian trickster and an ingenious, picaresque character from the Spanish Golden Century. The dialogue includes both legitimate Spanish and a Nahuatl dialect called *nahuate;* a kind of *lingua franca* or "a mixed dialect" that was spoken throughout Central America and southern Mexico. This dialect appeared after an early Nahuatl conversion to other Indian languages. According to D. G. Brinton, *nahuate* became "a common language for the mestizos". But, in this "mixed-dialect" that Mario Cajina Vega called "Espanáhuat," there is a prevailing Spanish syntax, using formal and grassroots lexicon.

4. Humorous poetry as resistance

Through language this play represents the perspective of the oppressed or the subordinate. Through its spontaneous humor, ingenious and biting sarcastic tone, the play works to critique the dominant discourse or rhetoric of the Spanish authorities. The objective is not to make people laugh or provoke catharsis; but instead it aims to use humor as a form of resistance. According to Barbara Harlow in her book *Resistance Literature* (1987), the oppressed uses a defensive humor as a means of resisting the oppressor. In her theoretical explanation, she states that the "big jerk" character comes from the oppressed classes, managing to survive with and among the others in the mist of difficulties.

Our theatrical play employs parodies, satarizing Spanish authorities. The courtesan and bureaucratic rhetoric is used by the following characters: Governor Tastuanes the royal representing the Spanish empire, the Bailiff or Alguacil in charge of keeping public order, the Royal Secretary (Clerk), and the Alderman (the Royal Assistant)—a member of the Indigenous Royal Council. Each of these characters are condemned and ridiculed in the play for being corrupt.

In Mr. Arellano's version in Spanish, there is a Muleteer—the assistant that carries the Güegüense's goods—who only speaks only three times, using eight syllables verses. This character is found in Walter Lehmann's manuscript, which was discovered and transcribed in Masaya in December 1984.

This rhetoric used to communicate at that time is questioned in the play by this one old man, the Güegüense, who deals in contraband items. However, the Güegüense is an indigenous, poor, and independent old man seeking social mobility. He is intent on joining the mainstream. His legitimate son Don Forsico supports the Güegüense in his aspiration, but his illegitimate son Don Ambrosio does not. After many discussions, they reached an agreement: Don Forsico marries the Governor's young daughter Doña Suche Malinche. At the end of the play, there is a masquerade party consistent with the farse or piece of clowning of the theatrical play.

5. Counterdiscourse of the oppressed

The Güegüense represents the counter-discourse of the oppressed in that it dramatizes the indigenous populations' confrontation with Spanish colonizers. It also effectively outlines the limits and failures of a Spanish colonial society. However while challenging the Spanish authorities, the play also paradoxically reaffirms the dominant position. The play attempts to portray an alternative to the social reality, reflecting Spanish ideological elements that The Güegüense faces in that place and time. (Terdiman, 1985: 76).

In spite of this, the theatrical piece gives voice to the oppressed, allowing the indigenous populations to express a yearning hope for equality. This play reveals a world and a culture that lead to an art masterpiece. Thus, *the Güegüense* cannot be thought of or studied in isolation, that is, as a simple fragment or passage. It should not be reduced to a literary text, scenic work, dance, linguistic document, or folkloric relic.

6. A triumph of culture over power

The Güegüense represents the triumph of the impoverished and oppressed over the oppressor. This triumph is achieved through mockery and malice. The play's expressions have double meanings, suggesting disdain to the sophistication and incisive sarcasm in the face of injustice, denouncing the servile attitude of authorities in the dialogues, including fantastic irony and no limits to imagination.

To summarize, it is a triumph of culture. Pablo Antonio Cuadra used to say that, "*The Güegüense* will always dance as long as poverty and political doublespeak prevail in our territory…[it is an example of the] victory of Culture over Power."

"The day and night are too short to talk about my father's vast riches," Don Forsico says in the play's dialogue. He supports hyperbolically Güegüense's statements, but his illegitimate son Don Ambrosio does not. The latter states that he is poor and for this reason, the Güegüense insults him using words like bad seed, brat with dead toad eyes, *etc.* On the other hand, Don Ambrosio had been frank and open, saying:

Good Heavens! Governor Tastuanes. I'm ashamed to talk about what this deceitful Güegüense does. He just waits for the night to fall, and he goes house-to-house, stealing what is left in the kitchens for him and my brother. Güegüense says that he has a chest of gold, but it is just an old basket full of lice; that he has a silken cot, but it is just a dirty old sleeping mat; that he has silk stockings, but they are an old pair of boots; that he has golden shoes, but they are worn out slippers without soles; that he has a golden rifle, but it is just the stick because the barrel was taken off."

The Güegüense talks for the people

The Güegüense is a pioneer representative work of the Mesoamerican dramatic art and the foundational piece in Nicaraguan literary tradition. It is a colonial critique, a humorous poetry, a counter-discourse of the oppressed, a proclamation of human equality, a work of art, and an example of the triumph of culture over power. As stated by renowned poet Rubén Darío, "The Güegüense talks for the people".

Translated by Rolando Ernesto Tellez

Characters:

Colonial Governor Tastuanes
Bailiff or Captain Chief Alguacil
Güegüence, father
Don Forcico, his older son
Don Ambrosio, his younger son
Doña Suche Malinche, governor's daughter
Royal Secretary

(Dancing)

1. Bailiff (addressed as Alguacil): I pray to God to protect you, Governor Tastuanes.

2. Governor: I pray to God to protect you, my son, Captain Chief Alguacil. Are you all right?

3. Bailiff: At your service (...)   **(he turns around dancing and talking about him)**

4. Bailiff (obsequious): I pray to God to protect you, Governor Tastuanes.

5. Governor: I pray to God to protect you, my son. **(in arrogant and imperative tone):** Stop in the Leading Men's quarters, the music, corruption, songs, ballads, Spanish dances, and entertainment, as requested in my Royal Court. Repeat and obey **(a resounding blow of percussion is heard).** In the first place, I have no golden table, no embroidered tablecloth, no golden inkstand, no pen of gold, no blotting paper made of gold. I just have white paper to sign the records of my Royal Court.

8. Bailiff: Stop the amusement at your Royal Court. **(obeying the explicit order)** First of all, you have no golden table, no embroidered tablecloth, no golden inkstand, no pen of gold, no blotting paper made of gold. You just have white paper to sign the records of my Royal Court.

9. Governor: My son, stop in the Leading Men's quarters, the music, corruption, songs, ballads, Spanish dances, and entertainment, as requested in my Royal Court, except those who got a permit from the patrol to enter my royal province.

10. Bailiff: At your service, Governor Tastuanes **(addressing the public).** I pray to God to protect the Leading Men that will not enjoy music, corruption, songs, ballads, Spanish dances, and entertainment, without the permit of Governor Tastuanes. **(They play music of the patrol, they dance. The Governor enters).**

10a. Bailiff (leading the patrol, but frustrated): It is very difficult to catch and bring this rascal called Güegüense.

(Music is played, the Governor and Bailiff danced, followed by the patrol. Meanwhile, they go back to the atrium).

11. Bailiff: Here we are, but the patrol isn't. **(Pause, talking about Güegüense).** Governor Tastuanes, this stubborn Güegüense is ashamed to show up in front of you. He's like the patrol's girdles in rags and tatters, with beaver hats smashed, and just a single saddle cloth or red cloak like those of that deceitful Güegüense.

12. Governor: My son, you must go and get that trickster, pimp, and charlatan. Grab or drag him by the tail, the legs, the nose **(making a particular gesture),** or any part of his body. May God help you, Captain Chief Alguacil **(leaving).**

15. Bailiff (follows the governor, yelling at him): At your service, Governor Tastuanes! **(Güegüense appears on the other side of the stage)**

16. Güegüense: Hey, guys! Is it a calf or colt that is tied behind by the tail, the legs, or the nose?

17. Don Ambrosio (pulling the mule train by using a rope): Güegüense, you're a big liar.

18. Güegüense (pretending not to hear): Don Forsico, are you talking to me?

19. Don Forsico (eating a fruit): No, father. Perhaps your ears are buzzing.

20. Güegüense: Don Ambrosio, are you talking to me?

21. Don Ambrosio (releasing the rope abruptly): Güegüense, who would talk to a scoundrel like you?

(Bailiff stealthily gets close to the group)

22.   Güegüense: Of course, you're a bad boy, you just fool around when everybody is working **(he listens to the Bailiff's steps)**. Now, who is it that wants to know my name?

23. Bailiff: A servant of Governor Tastuanes.

24. Güegüense: What? Which servant? The chocolate maker, the woman that washes the clothes or makes the bed for Governor Tastuanes?

25. Bailiff: None of the above, I mean a servant of Governor Tastuanes.

26. Güegüense (emphatic): So, which servant? The cook or maid of Governor Tastuanes?

27. Bailiff: Stop joking, none of them, rascal. **(shouting)** Neither cook nor maid of Governor Tastuanes. It is the Captain Chief Alguacil!

28. Güegüense: Ha! the Captain Chief Alguacil of Governor Tastuanes! Oh dear! **(ironic tone)** Captain Chief Alguacil, did you happen to leave your bludgeon at the quarters?

29. Bailiff (naughty, showing his genitalia): Perhaps, you can use my stick, Güegüense.

30. Güegüense (inviting him to sit on his legs): Better sit on mine, Captain Chief Alguacil.

31. Bailiff: You'd better sit down, Güegüense. **(long pause. Güegüense exchange looks in complicity and his children,).**

32. Güegüense (breaking the silence): Captain Chief Alguacil, what does Governor Tastuanes say?

33. Bailiff: He says you have to come and see him now. So, you must run and fly.

34. Güegüense (surprised): Run and fly? How does he expect an old poor man—full of aches and pains—to run and fly? Captain Chief Alguacil, and what does Governor Tastuanes' bird do?

35. Bailiff: Güegüense, that bird sings, making great gentlemen happy. And yours, what does it do?

36. Güegüense: It is curled into a ball. This is my consolation and my amusement. But (...) Running and flying? **(his head nodded in disagreement).**

37. Bailiff (emphatically): Yes, Güegüense, running and flying.

38. Güegüense (pretending not to hear): Hey boys! Are you talking to me?

39. Don Ambrosio: Güegüense, who's going to talk to a big liar like you?

40. Güegüense: Don Forsico, are you talking to me?

41. Don Forsico: No, father. Perhaps your ears are buzzing.

42. Güegüense: Is that right? **(pause)** Son, look after the store. I'll see if I can fly. **(trying to leave the stage).**

43. Bailiff: Just a moment, Güegüense. Which manners will you use to enter the royal presence of Governor Tastuanes?

44. Güegüense (returning) Which ones? Captain Chief Alguacil.

45. Bailiff: First, there should be a song or something like that, in order to amuse the Royal Court of Governor Tastuanes.

46. Güegüense: A song? Captain Chief Alguacil. Then, stop in the Leading Men's quarters, the music, corruption, songs, ballads, Spanish dances, and entertainment, and the like. Yes, Güegüense!
(both of them dance while the patrol joins the dance. Now, the set design is that of the Royal Court, and Güegüense and his sons and the Bailiff (Alguacil) enter. They begin to snoop around, getting in contact with the ladies-in-waiting of Suche Malinche, who is the Governor's daughter).

48. Bailiff: Now, we're at the right place.

49. Güegüense (energetic): Now, at the right jail?

50. Bailiff: At the right place

51. Güegüense: You mean jail work at the estate?

50. Bailiff: At the place.

51. Güegüense: At the place, so ... **(watching one of his sons flirting with the ladies, pretending not to see).** Captain Chief Alguacil, why don't you teach me the right manners and solemn courtesy to enter and leave the royal presence of Governor Tastuanes?

52. Bailiff: Of course! But nothing is for free. First, I need a salary.

53. Güegüense: (pretending not to hear) You mean salted fish? Hey boys, you got the salted fish we brought from Ometepe?

54. Don Forsico (having a good time): Here they are, father.

55. Don Ambrosio (entering lonely and disappointed): Nonsense, you got no salted fish, deceitful Güegüense!

56. Güegüense: What! You're a bad seed, you're ugly with dead toad eyes. **(Addressing the Bailiff)** I'm very sorry to tell you that we ran out of salted fish.

59. Bailiff: I don't care about salted fish, Güegüense.

60. Güegüense: Well, what do you want? Captain Chief Alguacil.

61. Bailiff: Naturally, money.

62. Güegüense: Ha! Natural honey? Hey guys, is there any natural honey that we brought from San Juan de Oriente?

63. Don Forsico: Here it is, father.

64. Güegüense: Captain Chief Alguacil, we got all kinds of honey. Which one do you want? Chunk honey or comb honey?

65. Bailiff: Neither one nor the other. I don't care for honey.

66. Güegüense: So, what do you want? Captain Chief Alguacil.

67. Bailiff: Hard currency.

68. Güegüense: Oh! You mean large hard curd. Boys, do we have that?

69. Don Forsico: No, father. My brother, Don Ambrosio, ate the curd.

70. Don Ambrosio: Güegüense, you are a trickster that got no curd.

71. Güegüense: What! Bad breed, you ate up all the curd. **(Addressing the Bailiff)** Captain Chief Alguacil, we ran out of the hard curd, because one of my boys eats like a hog, no leftovers.

72. Bailiff: I don't care for hard curd.

73. Güegüense: Well, Captain Alguacil, what do you want?

74. Bailiff: Güegüense, silver and gold doubloons.

75. Güegüense: Oh! Double. Hey boys, do you know how to double?

76. Don Forsico: Yes, father.

77. Güegüense: Go ahead boys, do it. God was with Captain Alguacil when we were talking and bargaining a moment ago, but now he is possessed by the devil.

78. Bailiff: Go to hell, Güegüense! I don't know and I don't care about doubling.

79. Güegüense: And what the hell do you want? Captain Chief Alguacil.

80. Bailiff: I'm talking about silver and gold coins or doubloons.

81. Güegüense: Silver and gold doubloons! Why don't you speak aloud? I'm old man and I can't hear. In these inland places, people know nothing of natural honey, salted fish, hard curd; they only understand ounces of gold and silver coins. Well, let's get down to business, how much do you want?

82. Bailiff: Everything you have in the store.

83. Güegüense: Everything, everything? You won't leave me anything?

84. Bailiff: Nothing, nothing, Güegüense.

85. Güegüense: How about a little bit?

86. Bailiff: Not even a little bit.

87. Güegüense (resigned attitude): Boys, you see how hard we've worked to feed another hungry man.

88. Don Forsico: So it is, father.

89. Don Ambrosio: That's what you deserve, deceitful Güegüense.

90. Güegüense: Get out now, you're a bad seed. You'll eat your damned fingernails.

91. Don Ambrosio: We'll eat them, Güegüense.

92. Güegüense (addressing the Bailiff): Then, put out your hands. **(He smiles, addressing the public)** A hungry person puts out two hands! Oh my! What long fingernails you have my friend, Captain Chief Alguacil! They look like those with the three-toed sloth! Oh there! A shot for these fingernails.

93. Bailiff: For your ass, Güegüense.

94. Güegüense (taking out a bag of coins): Well, here you go. One, two, three, four. Alas, my money! Boys, I've given four hundred and so pesos to my friend, Captain Chief Alguacil... But you, you can't even tell a 'real' from half a real **(currency used at that time).**

95. Bailiff: What! I understand all about them.

96. Güegüense: It goes like this **(he lies by mixing capacity measure with currency units):** the half of this half real is equivalent to two cuartillos; an octavo is two quarters; one quarter is two maravedis; and two maravedis is two blancos.

97. Bailiff: Well, Take them out! All of them!

98. Güegüense: Teach me first!

99. Bailiff: Well then, pay attention.

100. Güegüense: What are you waiting? Show me.

101. Bailiff (Reverentually as if teaching a lesson): I pray to God to protect Governor Tastuanes.

102. Güegüense: May God punish Governor Tastuanes.

103. Bailiff: May God protect Governor Tastuanes.

104. Güegüense: May God beat Governor Tastuanes.

105. Bailiff: You're a real joker, and you deserve a dozen whippings.

106. Güegüense: Dozen virgin chicks? Hey boys, do we have young virgin chicks? Here, Captain Chief Alguacil offers a dozen virgin chicks.

107. Don Forsico: Yes, father.

108. Güegüense: Captain Chief Alguacil, which chicks do you want? White ones or black ones?

109. Bailiff (snatched the rope from Don Ambrosio, whipping Güegüense twice): I whip you so you can understand, Güegüense!

110. Güegüense: Hey, stop it! Why did you do that? I paid you, and now you beat me. These are whippings, not virgin chicks.

111. Don Ambrosio: You deserve this. You're a trickster, Güegüense.

112. Don Forsico (seeing the Governor, Don Forsico moves away from the ladies): I pray to God to protect Governor Tastuanes, his servants and maids, the regular mayors of the Holy Brotherhood, the city councilors, registrars, notaries, and archivists, including close friends of Governor Tastuanes Royal Court.

113. Güegüense Friend Captain Chief Alguacil, I gave you my money for nothing, if I have to change my language. Man, shall I get a crafty book to learn courtesies from Spain, and recite them when I come before Governor Tastuanes?

114. Bailiff: That's right.

115. Güegüense: Then take a bow! **(the Governor enters suddenly and says)** I pray to God to protect you, Governor Tastuanes.

116. Governor: I pray to God to protect you, Güegüense. Are you all right?

117. Güegüense: I was ordered here. I come before you, your servants and maids, the regular mayors of the Holy Brotherhood, the city councilors, registrars, notaries, and archivists, including close friends of Governor Tastuanes Royal Court.

118. Governor: Well, what kind of permit you got to enter this royal venue?

119. Güegüense: Oh my God, Governor Tastuanes! Do I need a permit to unload something?

120. Governor: Yes, you need a permit.

121. Güegüense: Oh, good Lord, Governor Tastuanes! When I travelled and worked in all those faraway places—Veracruz, Verapaz, Antepeque, driving those mules and guiding my boys, one day, Don Forsico asked an innkeeper to bring us a dozen eggs. Then, we went on eating and unloading, and I ate again and I got the shits—unloaded—**(makes gestures as if defecating).** And there was no need to get a permit to do so, Governor Tastuanes.

122. Governor (reiterative and emphatic): Well, here you need a permit, Güegüense!

123. Güegüense: My Goodness, Governor Tastuanes! **(the stage changes showing the dreamy encounter of Güegüense with a girl, who sings from the window, and a group of ladies is listening to her):** I was coming down a straight street and a girl, who was sitting in a golden window, caught sight of me, and she told me: How handsome you are! How gallant you are! Güegüense, **(touching his belly),** something is in store for you here, Güegüense, Come in and sit down, Güegüense **(showing his genitalia).** There is sweetmeat here; **(touching his part)** there are lemons here. As I am a funny man, I jumped off and landed gracefully on the street. I had my riding cloak on, so full of ornaments that you could not tell what it was, covered with gold and silver to the ground. This is the way, a girl let me make "it," Governor Tastuanes. **(Music)**

124. Governor: But a girl can't give you a permit.

125. Güegüense: For Heaven's Sake, Governor Tastuanes! Let's not be silly. Let's be friends and let's get down to business with these clothes. First of all, here is a chest of gold, a chest of silver, clothes from Spain, smuggled clothes, bras, feather bloomers, silk stockings, golden shoes, beaver hats, stirrup straps of gold and silver lace, which will satisfy Governor Tastuanes.

126. Governor: Whether I like it or not, Güegüense, I can't tell with so many words coming out your mouth. Wouldn't it be better if your sons tell my Royal Court truthfully, whether or not you're wealthy—with abundant treasures?

127. Güegüense: Clever Governor Tastuanes, don't you already know?

128. Governor: I don't know.

129. Güegüense: In this case, friend Captain Chief Alguacil will stop here the music, corruption, songs, ballads, Spanish dances, and entertainment enjoyed by Leading Men, and Don Forsico will inform the Royal Court about this wealth and abundant treasures.

130. Governor: Gentleman Chief Alguacil, stop in the Leading Men's quarters, the music, corruption, songs, ballads, Spanish dances, and entertainment, so that Don Forsico will give a truthful account to my Royal Court about this imaginative Güegüense.

131. Bailiff: At your service, Governor Tastuanes. I pray to God to protect the Leading Men, and now they no longer will enjoy their music, corruption, songs and ballads, Spanish dances, and entertainment, because Don Forsico is going to tell the truth. **(music and dance)**

(later the Bailiff allows Don Forsico to talk with the Governor).

132. Don Forsico: I pray to God to protect you, Governor Tastuanes.

133. Governor: I pray to God to protect you, Don Forsico. Are you all right?

134. Don Forsico: I'm fine!

135. Governor: Then, Don Forsico. We've called you here to tell us the truth about Güegüense. Is he a very rich man, with a lot wealth, and beautiful treasures? He says he has a chest of gold, a chest of silver, gold doubloons, and silver coins. Tell me the truth, Don Forsico.

136. Don Forsico: Good Lord, Governor Tastuanes. The day and night are too short to talk about my father's vast riches. Is it enough, bloodsucker Governor Tastuanes?

137. Governor: It is not enough, Don Forsico. Perhaps all of that is part of your imagination. It is better to call your brother, Don Ambrosio, so that he tells my Royal Court the truth about Güegüense's vast riches and beautiful treasures.

138. Don Forsico: Governor Tastuanes, if Captain Chief Alguacil stops in the Leading Men's quarters, the music, corruption, songs, ballads, Spanish dances, and entertainment, then my younger brother, Don Ambrosio, will tell the truth.

139. Governor: Gentleman Captain Chief Alguacil. Have Don Ambrosio tell the truth about the presumed Güegüense's wealth and treasures.

140. Bailiff: At your service, Governor Tastuanes **(music and dance).**

141. Don Ambrosio: I pray to God to protect you, Governor Tastuanes.

142. Governor: I pray to God to protect you. Don Ambrosio, are you all right?

143. Don Ambrosio: I'm fine!

144. Governor: Don Ambrosio, you're going to tell me the truth about what Güegüense says. Is he a rich man? In the first place, Güegüense just boasts about a chest of gold, a chest of silver, clothes from Spain, smuggled clothes, bras, feather bloomers, silk stockings, golden shoes, beaver hats, stirrup straps of gold and silver lace, and beautiful treasures. Tell me the truth, Don Ambrosio.

145. Don Ambrosio: Good Heavens! Governor Tastuanes. I'm ashamed to talk about what this deceitful Güegüense does. He just waits for the night to fall, and he goes house-to-house, stealing what is left in the kitchens for him and my brother. Güegüense says that he has a chest of gold, but it is just an old basket full of lice; that he has a silken cot, but it is just a dirty old sleeping mat; that he has silk stockings, but they are an old pair of boots; that he has golden shoes, but they are worn out slippers without soles; that he has a golden rifle, but it is just the stick because the barrel was taken off.

146. Güegüense (addressing Don Forsico): What a shame to have a boy like that! Bigmouth, lying tongue! Don Forsico, break his head, since he is not my son. He damages my reputation.

147. Don Forsico (pushes his stepbrother): Get out of here, you bad seed! **(on the side of his father).** Governor Tastuanes, don't be shocked to hear this bigmouth. My father and I went to Mexico. When we returned, my mother was already pregnant, that's why my brother is such a bad seed (...)

148. Güegüense (proudly): Governor Tastuanes, are you now happy and satisfied with what Don Forsico has reported to the Royal Court, regarding my vast riches and beautiful treasures?

149. Governor: Whether or not I'm satisfied, I don't think the Royal Court is happy.

150. Güegüense (conceited): Clever Governor Tastuanes, aren't you already informed? Well, let friend Captain Chief Alguacil stop in the Leading Men's quarters, the music, corruption, songs, ballads, Spanish dances, and entertainment, to show Güegüense's store to the Royal Court.

151 Governor: Son, Captain Chief Alguacil, stop in the Leading Men's quarters, the music, corruption, songs, ballads, Spanish dances, and entertainment, so that this fake Güegüense shows his store or goods to the Royal Court.

152. Bailiff: At your service, Governor Tastuanes. I pray to God to protect the Leading Men that will no longer enjoy the music, corruption, songs, ballads, **(music)** Spanish dances, and entertainment, because this vain Güegüense will please the Royal Court by showing his goods. **(Güegüense and the boys dance around the stage with the tent or store).**

(The store is prepared)

153. Güegüense (loudmouth): I pray to God to protect you, Governor Tastuanes. Let me offer my store to the Royal Court. Guys, open the bundles and look at all these beautiful things. **(Addressing Governor Tastuanes)** a chest of gold, a chest of silver, bras, feather bloomers, silk stockings, golden shoes, beaver hats, stirrup straps of gold and silver lace, and beautiful treasures. **(As a lyric poet, referring to planet Venus that shines on his store)** Let me offer you this Morning Star that shines brightly on other side of the sea, **(he comes closer to be face to face with the Governor, being insolent and indecently showing his**

phallus) and this syringe of gold—an excellent medical tool—to cure the Royal Court of Governor Tastuanes.

154. Governor: Stick it in your butt, Güegüense.

155. Güegüense (rejecting Don Ambrosio): Ah! **(referring to Don Forsico)** My boy has so many trades. He's a jack of all trades all the way to his fingernails.

156. Governor: Dirt under his fingernails?

157. Güegüense: Governor Tastuanes, my son has been a sculptor, painter, actor, dancer, jester, foundry worker, bell-ringer.

158. Governor: But these are not permanent jobs.

159. Güegüense: He has also been a carpenter, maker of yokes, though of papaya tree, maker of plows, though of temple tree wood. This should have satisfied clever Governor Tastuanes.

160. Governor: Güegüense, I'm not yet satisfied. You'd better ask Don Forsico to tell the truth about so many trades.

161. Güegüense: Then, friend Captain Chief Alguacil, stop in the Leading Men's quarters, the music, corruption, songs, ballads, Spanish dances, and entertainment for Don Forsico to give a truthful account of his trades to the Royal Court.

162. Bailiff: Right away, Güegüense.
(music, Bailiff takes Don Forsico to the Governor)

163. Don Forsico: Governor Tastuanes, I'm a jack of all trades all the way to my fingernails.

164. Governor (exclaiming, offensive): Don Forsico, that must be dirt under your fingernails!

165. Don Forsico (repeating what his father said): Governor Tastuanes, I have been a sculptor, painter, actor, dancer, jester, foundry worker, bell-ringer, flyer **(miming how a blackbird flies)**.

166. Governor: This is not satisfactory yet. Don Forsico, you must know some clever tap dance or zapateado to amuse the Royal Court.

167. Don Forsico: Oh my, Governor Tastuanes! If friend Captain Chief Alguacil stops in the Leading Men's quarters, the music, corruption, songs, ballads, Spanish dances, and entertainment, the Royal Court will enjoy running dances and other clever dances.

168. Governor: Son, Captain Chief Alguacil, stop in the Leading Men's quarters, the music, corruption, songs, ballads, Spanish dances, and entertainment to please this phony Güegüense.

169. Bailiff: At your service, Sir. Leading men, stop the music, corruption, songs, ballads, Spanish dances, and entertainment for this big clown, Güegüense, to amuse the Royal Court.
(first ballet with running dance, and he talks)

170. Güegüense: Are you satisfied now that my children have amused the Royal Court with dances like tap dance?

171. Governor: I'm not satisfied, Güegüense. I won't know until Don Forsico and Don Ambrosio can do something to amuse the Royal Court.

172. Güegüense: (ironic) Don't you see? Governor Tastuanes,

173. Governor: I don't know, Güegüense.

174. Güegüense: That friend Captain Chief Alguacil, stop in the Leading Men's quarters, the music, corruption, songs, ballads, Spanish dances, and entertainment, so that Don Forsico and Don Ambrosio amuse the Royal Court.

175. Bailiff (showing his servile attitude): At your service, Governor Tastuanes. **(Güegüense and the two boys, along with the Bailiff, dance again).**

176. Güegüense: Governor Tastuanes, Are you satisfied to see that they can tap dance to amuse the Royal Court?

177. Governor: I am not satisfied.

178. Güegüense: Can Governor Tastuanes find out if Don Forsico and Don Ambrosio can tap dance to the tune of St. Martin to amuse the Royal Court?

179. Governor: I don't know yet, Güegüense. Son, **(nodding to the Bailiff)** Captain Chief Alguacil, stop in the Leading Men's quarters, the music, corruption, songs, ballads, Spanish dances, and entertainment for the sons—of this conceited Güegüense—to amuse the Royal Court, to the tune of St. Martin.

180. Governor: Güegüense, I am now satisfied you can tap dance to amuse the Royal Court.

181. Güegüense: Whether or not I'm satisfied, Governor Tastuanes, perhaps, my friend Captain Chief Alguacil may amuse the Royal Court with Puerto Rican music.

182. Governor (addressing the Bailiff): My son, Captain Chief Alguacil, stop in the Leading Men's quarters, the continuous parties, so that you can amuse the Royal Court with Puerto Rican music. **(Bailiff hesitating and not very happy)**

(Puerto Rican music is played, and the Bailiff and the patrol dance).

183. Governor: Alright, Güegüense. I'm now pleased with the dances that have amused the Royal Court.

184. Güegüense: But I'm not satisfied, Governor Tastuanes, because some move backward and others move forward.

185. Governor: I don't care about that. I want to know if you can perform the Macho-Raton dance to amuse the Royal Court.

186. Güegüense (assuming a position of authority): Governor Tastuanes and my good friend Captain Chief Alguacil, stop the continuous parties, in order to amuse the Royal Court with the dance or tap dance steps of the male mules. Hey boys! What about the mules? **(referring to the masked male mules)**

187. Don Forsico: Here they are, father.

(the tune of Macho-Raton or Valona (alternating song and recital) is played for the boys to dance on the back of the mules).

188. **Güegüense:** Governor Tastuanes, are you now satisfied with the tap dance, final steps, and prance of the small mule or Macho-Raton?

189. **Governor:** Not yet, Güegüense. **(a group of ladies parades, and Dona Suche Malinche is among them).**

190. **Güegüense:** Then, Governor Tastuanes, Why don't we make a deal and contract with this penniless rascal **(referring to Don Forsico)**? Let's marry Doña Suche Malinche with him, and then we're even.

191. **Governor (scornfully):** Güegüense, what are you suggesting?

192. **Güegüense (justifying himself):** I'm just suggesting, Governor Tastuanes.

192a. **Governor:** How dare you suggest such thing?

192b. **Güegüense:** Just as I told you, Governor Tastuanes.

192c. **Governor:** With Don Forsico?

192d. **Güegüense:** And Doña Suche Malinche!

192e. **Governor:** You aim too high!

192f. **Güegüense (with certainty):** To close the deal, let's sign the contract!

193. **Governor (hesitating):** Son, Captain Chief Alguacil, stop the work in the quarters of the Royal Secretary, and let him obey the order to enter my royal presence, accompanied by Doña Suche Malinche. **(Bailiff goes to talk with the Royal Secretary)**

194. **Bailiff:** I pray to God to protect you, Mr. Royal Secretary.

195. **Royal Secretary:** I pray to God to protect you, Chief Alguacil. **(Sickly-sweet).** Are you all right?

196. Bailiff (in denial): Mr. Royal Secretary, I was ordered here to make you obey the order of showing up before Governor Tastuanes. Doña Suche Malinche will have to come with you.

197. Royal Secretary: Gentleman Captain Chief, go ahead and stop the continuous parties of the Leading Men, to obey the order and bring Doña Suche Malinche.

198. Bailiff: Right away, Mr. Royal Secretary.
(They play the Rujero—the ladies' song, and they dance, going around in circles)

199. Secretary: I pray to our merciful God to protect you, Governor Tastuanes.

200. Governor: I pray to God to protect you, Mr. Royal Secretary. Are you all right?

201. Secretary (submissive): Here we are. Both of us, Doña Suche Malinche and I, are ready to obey orders.

202. Governor (talking softly): Well, Mr. Secretary, here is the deal, go ahead and marry this conceited and supposedly rich Güegüense with Doña Suche Malinche.

203. Secretary (flatterer): Governor Tastuanes, first he needs a dowry for the bride. This dowry consists of a skirt from China, a bra, a feather bloomer, silk stockings, golden shoes, beaver hat, in order to be your son-in-law. **(When Güegüense listens to this, he intends to leave the stage).**
(the Secretary returns to his place, dancing with the Bailiff).

204. Governor: Ah! Güegüense, I'm pleased you chose a wife.

205. Güegüense: What? Maybe a daughter-in-law

206. Governor: Wife, Güegüense.

207. Güegüense: No, daughter-in-law, I made no contract with you. Maybe, you're referring to my boy.

208. Governor: I don't mind.

209. Güegüense (evasive): Hey son, what deal or contract do you have with Governor Tastuanes?

210. Don Forsico: I'm getting married, father.

211. Güegüense: You are getting married? You're so young and naïve. Why do you dare get married?

212. Don Forsico: Yes, father.

213. Güegüense: Son, and who am I going to live with?

214. Don Forsico: My younger brother, Don Ambrosio.

215. Güegüense: That pale man will not look after me!

216. Don Ambrosio (enthusiastically): I want to get married too!

217. Güegüense: You're good for that. **(to the public)** Don Ambrosio also wishes to choose a wife. **(addressing Don Forsico and pointing to one of the two ladies)** Look, what a gorgeous maid!

218. Don Forsico: I don't like that one, father.

219. Güegüense: Son, why not?

220. Don Forsico (unsatisfied): Because she's too skinny, father.

221. Güegüense: Any iguana would be skinny after laying eggs. Who did that to her?

222. Don Forsico: My little brother Don Ambrosio, father.

223. Güegüense: You see? This brat with dead toad eyes is good for that. **(addressing Don Forsico and pointing to another lady).** Son, there's an exquisite girl! Take a look!

224. Don Forsico: But, she's already pregnant, father.

225. Güegüense: Son, who got her pregnant?

226. Don Forsico: My little brother Don Ambrosio.

227. Güegüense: Don Ambrosio, how did you make her belly grow?

228. Don Ambrosio: By sleeping with you, Güegüense.

229. Güegüense: Shut up, you're a bad seed. **(pointing to Doña Suche Malinche)** Son, look at this other beautiful lady!

230. Don Forsico (satisfied): I like this one, father.

231. Güegüense: You know how to choose a mate, right? But, you don't know how to find a good machete to cut the grass very well.

232. Don Forsico: I also know how to do that, father.

233. Güegüense: Governor Tastuanes, shall we close the deal, by signing the contract?

234. Governor: OK, let's sign it.

235. Güegüense: Governor Tastuanes... That's it, **(weeping)** I feel I've lost my boy.

236. Governor: I don't care about that.
(The marriage takes place)

237. Governor: Son, Captain Chief Alguacil, spread the news in this province that this joker Güegüense will treat the Royal Court to two barrels of Spanish wine.

238. Royal Secretary: Just a moment, Captain Chief Alguacil. **(addressing Güegüense)** Distinguished and bold friend, in the name of the Royal Court, we congratulate you, giving Doña Suche Malinche. Your son, Don Forsico, will enjoy her!

239. Bailiff: Ah! Güegüense, it is known in the Royal Province of Governor Tastuanes that you are to obey him. And you have to give two barrels of Spanish wine for a toast.

240. Güegüense: Hey boys! We are in trouble now. It's a fine thing to get married, but now we have a big job to do. The wedding ceremony is coming, but we don't have provisions **(to the Bailiff).** Friend Captain Chief Alguacil, where did you put those barrels of wine?

241. Bailiff: I don't know what you're talking about. That's your job.

242. Güegüense: Boys, you see? Marriage forces us to seek a yoke of oxen and a cart.

243. Bailiff: I'm not interested in neither an oxen nor a cart. We just want two barrels of Spanish wine and make a toast with Governor Tastuanes Royal Court.

244. Güegüense: Son, you see? This marriage has got me in trouble. You've already heard what Governor Tastuanes asked for. He wants two barrels of Spanish wine for a toast. Son, dare you seek the barrels of wine?

245. Don Forsico: I don't know where to get them, father.

246. Güegüense: If you're bold enough to choose woman, **(addressing Don Ambrosio)** Don Ambrosio, dare you seek two barrels of Spanish wine?

247. Don Ambrosio: I don't know where to get them.

248. Güegüense: What are you good for, you're a bad seed. **(addressing Don Forsico)** Well, dare you seek the wine?

249. Don Forsico: No, father.

250. Güegüense: Whatever I have to do, I'll get two barrels of Spanish wine.

251. Don Forsico: Don't go, father. I've already got two barrels of Spanish wine.

252. Güegüense: Son, where did you get them?

253. Don Forsico (showing a gesture that he stole them): At a friend's house.

254. Güegüense: Who taught you how to steal from a friend?

255. Don Forsico: You did, father.

256. Güegüense (addressing oneself to the public): Shut up, boy. What will people say if they know that I taught you how to steal from a friend?

257. Don Ambrosio: Well, isn't it true that you taught your son bad habits?

258. Güegüense: Get out! You're a bad seed. **(addressing the Bailiff)** Friend Captain Chief Alguacil, we've already got two barrels of Spanish wine. Isn't there a mule to carry the barrels?

259. Bailiff: You see? This is the famous rich man!

260. Güegüense (confidently): Friend Captain Chief Alguacil, I sure am a rich man! My own mules have worked so hard that they are exhausted. **(addressing the boys)** Hey guys! What about the mules?

261. Don Forsico: There they are, father.
(they take the mules, turning and dancing with them).

262. Don Forsico: The male mules are now driven up, father.

263. Güegüense: Shriveled? They must be cold.

264. Don Forsico: The male mules are being driven up.

265. Güegüense: Living studs? Weren't these male mules castrated?

266. Don Forsico: I said the mules are driven up, father.

267. Güegüense: Were the mules gathered? Speak loudly to me. Where are the mules?

268. Don Forsico: Here they are, father.

269. Güegüense: Son, which is the leading mule?

270. Don Forsico: This is the old mule, father.

271. Güegüense: How about this other mule?

272. Don Forsico: That's the skinny one from Oaxaca.

273. Güegüense: And this other mule?

274. Don Forsico: This is the mad mule.

275. Güegüense: And that other one?

276. Don Forsico: That's the orphan calf.

277. Güegüense: Boys, are they harnessed?

278. Don Forsico: No, father. You have to harness them.

279. Güegüense (resigned attitude): Why does this old man have to do everything?

280. Don Forsico: It's better this way, father.

281. Güegüense: Son, is the wound of this mule cured?

282. Don Forsico: Oh yes, father.

283. Güegüense: And this other mule, is it cured too?

284. Don Forsico: Yes, father.

285. Güegüense (showing the penis of the animal): This is not healed up. The shaft is swollen in the front. Son, where did its shaft get swollen?

286. Don Forsico: At the pasture, father.

287. Güegüense: That's what it deserved for running from one pasture to another. Son, and is the sore on the buttocks of this mule all right?

288. Don Forsico: Sure, father.

289. Güegüense: This blood blister is not all right. Young son, this swelling is now beneath the legs and it's very swollen. Son, burst it open!

290. Don Forsico: Father. You'd better open it.

291. Güegüense: Son, it will burst by itself. Now, what do we do?

292. Don Forsico: Pick up the bundle.

293. Güegüense: Warming up to juggle?

294. Don Forsico: Pick up the bundle.

295. Güegüense: Ah! The bundle. Where's the bundle?

296. Don Forsico: Here you are, father.

297. Güegüense: Oh, when I was a boy I was so happy and full of life. I remember when I used to lift those bundles of guavas in those plains of the indigenous people in Diriomo. Boys, those days are over!

298. Bailiff (interrupting): Hurry up, Güegüense.

299. Güegüense: Captain Chief Alguacil, are you taking me to prison? Why are you doing this?

300. Bailiff: I just said, hurry up.

301. Güegüense: Let me remember the old good days: this makes me feel so good! **(yelling at his sons)**: Ah! Boys, are we going backwards or forwards?

302. Don Forsico: Forwards, father.

303. Güegüense: Come on, boys, let's go! **(the boys mount the mules)**

304. Güegüense: Sons, isn't there a servile guy out there to toast the Royal Court of Governor Tastuanes?

305. Don Forsico (referring to the Bailiff): Of course, father.

306. Güegüense: Governor Tastuanes, let me treat you to some Spanish wine.

307. Governor: OK, Güegüense.

308. Güegüense (addressing the Secretary): Mr. Royal Secretary, will you join me in a toast, by drinking Spanish wine?

309. Secretary: All right.

310. Güegüense (addressing the Governor): Mister Royal Main Servant, with this wine, let's propose a toast to Spain!

311. Governor: Very well!

312. Güegüense: Mister Main Servant, with this booze, here's to Spain!

313. Bailiff: Go ahead, Güegüense.

314. Güegüense: Guys, with this stolen wine, let's get drunk and have fun!